Mastering Your Destiny: Personal Development Goals for All

Amelie Dubois

Copyright © [2023]

Author: Amelie Dubois

Title: Mastering Your Destiny: Personal Development Goals for All

All rights reserved. No part of this book may be reproduced or transmitted in any form or by any means, electronic or mechanical, including photocopying, recording, or by any information storage and retrieval system, without permission in writing from the author.

This book is a product of [Publisher's Amelie Dubois]

ISBN:

TABLE OF CONTENTS

Chapter 1: Understanding Personal Development Goals

The Importance of Personal Development Goals

In life, it is essential to have a clear sense of purpose and direction. Setting personal development goals is a powerful way to ensure that you are constantly growing, improving, and moving towards the life you desire. Whether you want to excel in your career, improve your relationships, or enhance your overall well-being, having personal development goals is crucial.

First and foremost, personal development goals provide you with a roadmap. They act as a guide, helping you prioritize your actions and make decisions that align with your long-term vision. Without goals, you may find yourself aimlessly wandering through life, lacking focus and direction. By setting clear objectives, you create a sense of purpose and motivation that propels you forward.

Moreover, personal development goals allow you to measure your progress. They provide you with tangible benchmarks against which you can assess your growth and development. This not only helps you stay accountable but also provides a sense of fulfillment and achievement as you reach each milestone. By tracking your progress, you can identify areas where you need to improve and make necessary adjustments to stay on track.

Setting personal development goals also promotes self-awareness. As you reflect on your aspirations and desires, you gain a deeper understanding of yourself. This self-awareness is essential for personal growth, as it allows you to identify your strengths, weaknesses, and areas for improvement. By acknowledging your limitations, you can seek opportunities to learn and develop new skills that will help you overcome obstacles and achieve your goals.

Furthermore, personal development goals foster a growth mindset. They encourage you to embrace challenges and view failures as opportunities for learning and growth. By setting ambitious but achievable goals, you push yourself outside of your comfort zone and expand your capabilities. This fosters resilience, perseverance, and a continuous desire for self-improvement.

Lastly, personal development goals empower you to take control of your life. They provide a sense of autonomy and ownership, as you actively work towards the life you envision. By taking charge of your personal growth, you become the driver of your destiny and can create a life that aligns with your values and aspirations.

In conclusion, personal development goals are vital for everyone, regardless of their background or aspirations. They provide a roadmap, measure progress, promote self-awareness, cultivate a growth mindset, and empower individuals to take control of their lives. By setting personal development goals, you can unlock your full potential and create a life filled with purpose, fulfillment, and success.

Identifying Your Current Life Situation

In order to embark on a journey of personal development and goal setting, it is crucial to first understand your current life situation. This subchapter of "Mastering Your Destiny: Personal Development Goals for All" is designed to help you gain clarity about where you stand in life and lay the foundation for achieving your aspirations.

Life is a complex tapestry of experiences, relationships, and circumstances. It is only by assessing and acknowledging our current situation that we can determine the direction we want to move in. This self-reflection process allows us to identify areas of improvement, strengths to leverage, and obstacles to overcome.

To start, take a deep breath and create a quiet space for introspection. Reflect on various aspects of your life: career, relationships, health, finances, personal growth, and any other areas that hold significance for you. Ask yourself questions like:

1. Where am I currently in my career? Am I satisfied or do I feel stuck?

2. How are my relationships with family, friends, and significant others? Are they fulfilling or in need of work?

3. What is my physical and mental well-being like? Do I prioritize self-care and maintain a healthy lifestyle?

4. What is my financial situation? Am I managing my finances effectively or do I need to make improvements?

5. Do I feel a sense of purpose and personal growth? Am I challenging myself to learn and develop new skills?

As you answer these questions, be honest with yourself. This is not a judgmental exercise, but rather an opportunity to gain insight into where you are currently and where you want to go. Take note of any patterns or recurring themes that emerge, both positive and negative.

Remember that everyone's life situation is unique. Your journey is yours alone, and comparing yourself to others will only hinder your progress. Embrace your own reality and focus on what you can do to improve your circumstances.

By identifying your current life situation, you lay the groundwork for setting meaningful goals and creating a roadmap towards personal development. This self-awareness will empower you to make informed decisions and take intentional actions. So, take the time to understand yourself and your life situation, and get ready to embark on a transformative journey towards mastering your destiny.

Setting Clear and Specific Goals

In the pursuit of personal development, setting clear and specific goals is paramount. Whether you are an aspiring entrepreneur, a dedicated student, or simply seeking self-improvement, having well-defined objectives can provide you with a sense of direction and purpose. This subchapter aims to guide you in mastering the art of setting clear and specific goals, helping you pave your path towards success.

Goals are the driving force behind our actions and achievements. They provide us with a sense of purpose and motivate us to push beyond our limits. However, setting vague or broad goals often leads to confusion and lack of progress. To maximize your chances of success, it is crucial to set clear and specific goals that are aligned with your passions, values, and long-term aspirations.

When setting goals, it is essential to be specific. Instead of saying, "I want to start a business," articulate your goal as, "I want to launch a successful online clothing store specializing in sustainable fashion within the next year." By specifying what you want to achieve, you create a clear target to work towards, allowing you to develop a focused plan of action.

Furthermore, setting clear goals provides you with a benchmark for measuring progress. Instead of feeling overwhelmed by a vague goal, you can break it down into smaller, manageable tasks. This allows you to track your progress and celebrate milestones along the way, boosting your motivation and confidence.

To ensure your goals are both clear and specific, consider the SMART criteria. SMART stands for Specific, Measurable, Achievable, Relevant, and Time-bound. By applying these principles, you can create goals that are well-defined, realistic, and time-sensitive. For example, instead of saying, "I want to get fit," a SMART goal would be, "I want to lose 10 pounds and improve my cardiovascular fitness by running 5 kilometers in under 30 minutes within the next three months."

Remember, setting clear and specific goals is not just about writing them down; it also involves creating an action plan and staying committed. Break your goals into actionable steps and set deadlines for each milestone. Regularly review and adjust your goals as needed, ensuring they remain relevant and aligned with your evolving aspirations.

In conclusion, mastering the art of setting clear and specific goals is a fundamental aspect of personal development. By being specific, utilizing the SMART criteria, and creating a well-defined action plan, you can transform your aspirations into tangible achievements. Embrace the power of setting clear and specific goals, and watch as you take control of your destiny, one step at a time.

Creating a Personal Development Plan

In the journey of life, setting personal development goals is crucial for achieving success and fulfillment. A personal development plan serves as a roadmap to guide you towards self-improvement and actualizing your potential. By taking control of your destiny through a well-structured plan, you can unlock your true potential and live a more purposeful and rewarding life.

Begin by understanding your current situation and identifying areas for improvement. Reflect on your strengths, weaknesses, passions, and values. Evaluate your goals and aspirations in various aspects of life, including career, relationships, health, and personal growth. This introspection will help you gain clarity about what you truly want to achieve and what steps you need to take to get there.

Next, set SMART goals – Specific, Measurable, Achievable, Relevant, and Time-bound. Break down your long-term goals into smaller, manageable milestones. This way, you can track your progress and stay motivated along the way. Remember to prioritize your goals based on their importance and urgency.

To ensure your personal development plan is effective, it is essential to have a clear action plan. Define specific actions and strategies you will undertake to achieve each goal. Create a timeline and allocate resources, such as time, effort, and finances, accordingly. Incorporate regular self-reflection and evaluation to assess your progress and make necessary adjustments.

Furthermore, seek out opportunities for growth and learning. Engage in activities that align with your goals and interests. Attend seminars, workshops, or enroll in courses that can enhance your skills and knowledge. Embrace new experiences, take calculated risks, and step out of your comfort zone. Surround yourself with like-minded individuals who can support and inspire you on your personal development journey.

Additionally, cultivate healthy habits that promote well-being and personal growth. Prioritize self-care by taking care of your physical, mental, and emotional health. Incorporate mindfulness practices, exercise regularly, maintain a balanced diet, and get enough sleep. Develop a habit of continuous learning by reading books, listening to podcasts, or engaging in intellectual discussions.

Finally, remain adaptable and resilient in the face of challenges. Understand that setbacks are a natural part of the growth process. Embrace them as opportunities for learning and personal development. Maintain a positive mindset, persevere, and stay motivated even during tough times.

Remember, personal development is a lifelong journey. Review and revise your personal development plan periodically to ensure it remains relevant and aligned with your evolving aspirations. By creating and following a personal development plan, you can take control of your destiny and live a purposeful and fulfilling life. Start today and embark on a transformative journey towards mastering your destiny.

Chapter 2: Building a Positive Mindset

The Power of Positive Thinking

In our pursuit of personal development goals, one of the most powerful tools we possess is the ability to embrace positive thinking. It is a mindset that has the potential to transform our lives and unlock our true potential. The power of positive thinking lies in its ability to shape our thoughts, emotions, and actions, ultimately leading us towards success and fulfillment.

Positive thinking is not about denying the challenges and obstacles we face; it is about approaching them with optimism and confidence. When we cultivate a positive mindset, we train ourselves to see opportunities where others see roadblocks. We become resilient in the face of adversity, knowing that every setback is merely a stepping stone towards our goals.

The impact of positive thinking on our personal development journey cannot be understated. It has been scientifically proven that positive thoughts generate positive emotions, which in turn influence our behavior and outcomes. By adopting a positive attitude, we attract positive experiences and individuals into our lives, creating a ripple effect that propels us towards our desired goals.

Moreover, positive thinking has a profound effect on our mental and physical well-being. Research has shown that individuals who maintain a positive outlook on life are more likely to have better overall health, lower stress levels, and increased longevity. By focusing on the positive aspects of our lives, we activate the body's natural healing mechanisms and boost our immune system.

To harness the power of positive thinking, it is essential to cultivate a daily practice of gratitude and mindfulness. By expressing gratitude for the blessings in our lives, we shift our attention away from what is lacking and towards abundance. Mindfulness allows us to observe our thoughts and emotions without judgment, enabling us to choose positive perspectives and responses.

In the pursuit of our personal development goals, we must also surround ourselves with positivity. This includes seeking out supportive individuals who uplift and inspire us, as well as engaging in activities that bring us joy and fulfillment. By creating a positive environment, we create fertile ground for our personal growth and success.

In conclusion, the power of positive thinking is a force that can guide us towards our personal development goals. By embracing a positive mindset, we unlock our true potential, attract positive experiences, and improve our overall well-being. Let us embrace the power of positive thinking and create a life filled with abundance, joy, and success.

Overcoming Limiting Beliefs

In our journey towards personal development and achieving our goals, one of the biggest obstacles we often encounter is our own limiting beliefs. These beliefs are like invisible chains that hold us back from reaching our full potential. They are the negative thoughts and self-doubt that whisper in our ears, telling us that we are not capable or deserving of success.

However, it is important to understand that these limiting beliefs are not based on reality. They are merely stories that we have told ourselves over time, based on past experiences or outside influences. The good news is that we have the power to change these beliefs and break free from their grasp.

The first step in overcoming limiting beliefs is to become aware of them. Take a moment to reflect on the thoughts and beliefs that have been holding you back. Are you constantly telling yourself that you are not smart enough, talented enough, or worthy enough? Write down these beliefs and acknowledge that they are just beliefs, not truths.

Once you have identified your limiting beliefs, it is time to challenge them. Ask yourself, "Is this belief serving me? Is it helping me to achieve my goals?" More often than not, the answer will be no. Replace these negative beliefs with positive affirmations. For example, if you believe that you are not smart enough, replace it with "I am intelligent and capable of learning anything I set my mind to."

Visualize yourself as the person you want to become, free from these limiting beliefs. Imagine yourself achieving your goals and living the life you desire. This visualization will help rewire your subconscious mind and reinforce positive beliefs.

Surround yourself with positive influences. Seek out mentors, friends, or books that inspire and motivate you. Surrounding yourself with people who believe in your potential will empower you to overcome your limiting beliefs.

Finally, take action. Break through the barriers of your comfort zone and challenge yourself to step outside of it. Each small step towards your goals will reinforce the belief that you are capable of achieving them.

Remember, overcoming limiting beliefs is a process that requires patience and persistence. It is not something that can be accomplished overnight. However, with dedication and a belief in yourself, you can break free from the chains of these beliefs and create the life you deserve.

In conclusion, overcoming limiting beliefs is crucial for personal development and achieving our goals. By becoming aware of these beliefs, challenging them, visualizing success, surrounding ourselves with positive influences, and taking action, we can break free from their grasp and create a life of fulfillment and success. Don't let your limiting beliefs hold you back any longer; take the first step towards mastering your destiny today.

Cultivating Self-Confidence

Self-confidence is a powerful trait that can positively impact every aspect of our lives. It empowers us to pursue our dreams, take risks, and overcome obstacles. However, building self-confidence is not an overnight process; it requires dedication, self-reflection, and consistent effort. In this subchapter, we will explore various strategies and techniques to help you cultivate self-confidence and achieve your personal development goals.

1. Embrace self-acceptance: Start by accepting yourself for who you are, including your strengths and weaknesses. Recognize that nobody is perfect and that everyone has their own unique qualities. Embracing self-acceptance allows you to let go of negative self-judgment and focus on your growth.

2. Set realistic goals: Setting achievable goals is crucial for building self-confidence. Break down your larger goals into smaller, manageable steps. Celebrate each milestone you achieve along the way, as this will boost your confidence and motivation.

3. Challenge negative self-talk: Pay attention to your inner dialogue and challenge any negative thoughts or self-doubt. Replace them with positive affirmations and reminders of your past successes. Surround yourself with supportive and uplifting individuals who believe in your abilities.

4. Step out of your comfort zone: Growth and self-confidence are often found outside of our comfort zones. Take calculated risks and push yourself to try new experiences. Each time you conquer a fear or overcome a challenge, your confidence will soar.

5. Practice self-care: Taking care of your physical and mental well-being is essential for cultivating self-confidence. Engage in activities that bring you joy, such as exercise, meditation, or hobbies. Prioritize self-care to maintain a positive mindset and a healthy level of self-esteem.

6. Learn from failure: Failure is not a reflection of your worth; it is an opportunity for growth. Embrace failures as valuable lessons and use them to improve yourself. By learning from your mistakes, you will become more resilient and confident in your abilities.

7. Seek continuous learning: Strive to expand your knowledge and skills in areas that interest you. Attend workshops, read books, or enroll in courses that will enhance your expertise. The more you learn, the more confident you will become in your abilities.

Remember, self-confidence is not a destination; it is a lifelong journey. Embrace the process and celebrate every step forward, no matter how small. By cultivating self-confidence, you will unlock your full potential, achieve your goals, and master your destiny.

Practicing Gratitude and Mindfulness

In our fast-paced and often chaotic world, it can be easy to lose sight of our goals and become overwhelmed by the demands of daily life. However, by incorporating gratitude and mindfulness into our daily routines, we can regain control of our destinies and find true fulfillment.

Gratitude is the practice of intentionally acknowledging and appreciating the positive aspects of our lives. It is about recognizing the blessings we have, both big and small, and expressing gratitude for them. By cultivating a mindset of gratitude, we shift our focus from what is lacking to what we already have, fostering a sense of contentment and joy.

Practicing gratitude on a regular basis can have profound effects on our well-being and overall happiness. Research has shown that individuals who regularly express gratitude experience lower levels of stress, enhanced relationships, improved physical health, and increased resilience. By consciously acknowledging the good in our lives, we can develop a more positive outlook and attract more positivity into our existence.

Mindfulness, on the other hand, is the practice of being fully present in the current moment without judgment. It involves paying attention to our thoughts, emotions, and physical sensations in a non-reactive manner. By practicing mindfulness, we develop greater self-awareness and enhance our ability to respond to situations instead of reacting impulsively.

Incorporating mindfulness into our lives allows us to break free from the autopilot mode that often dominates our thoughts and actions. It helps us become more attuned to our inner desires and aspirations, enabling us to align our goals with our authentic selves. When we are mindful, we can make intentional choices that lead us towards our desired outcomes, rather than being driven by external influences.

By combining gratitude and mindfulness, we can create a powerful framework for personal development and goal achievement. When we approach our goals with a grateful mindset, we appreciate the journey and the lessons it brings, rather than solely focusing on the end result. This not only enhances our motivation and perseverance but also allows us to savor the present moment and find joy in the process.

In "Mastering Your Destiny: Personal Development Goals for All," we explore practical strategies for cultivating gratitude and mindfulness in our everyday lives. Through insightful exercises, guided meditations, and real-life examples, this subchapter aims to empower every individual with the tools needed to harness the power of gratitude and mindfulness in achieving their goals.

Regardless of your background or aspirations, embracing gratitude and mindfulness will transform your life. It will enable you to live with intention, find greater fulfillment, and ultimately master your own destiny. Start your journey towards personal growth and goal attainment today by incorporating the practices of gratitude and mindfulness into your life.

Chapter 3: Developing Emotional Intelligence

Understanding Emotions and Their Impact

Emotions are an essential part of the human experience. They influence our thoughts, behaviors, and overall well-being. In the journey of personal development, it is crucial to understand emotions and their impact on our lives. By recognizing and managing our emotions effectively, we can take charge of our destiny and achieve our goals.

Emotions can be both positive and negative, and they often arise as a response to the situations we encounter in life. Joy, love, excitement, and passion are examples of positive emotions that can motivate us and fuel our ambition to reach our goals. On the other hand, negative emotions like fear, anger, sadness, and frustration can hinder our progress and hold us back from achieving what we desire.

Understanding the root causes of our emotions is the first step towards emotional mastery. By becoming aware of the triggers and patterns that elicit certain emotional responses, we can gain control over our reactions. This self-awareness allows us to choose how we respond to situations, rather than being driven solely by our emotions.

Emotions can have a profound impact on our decision-making process. When we are overwhelmed by negative emotions, our judgment becomes clouded, and we may make impulsive choices that are not aligned with our long-term goals. By learning to regulate our emotions, we can make more rational and informed decisions that support our personal development journey.

Furthermore, emotions influence our relationships with others. Our ability to empathize, understand, and connect with people is greatly influenced by our emotional intelligence. By developing emotional intelligence, we can enhance our communication skills, build stronger relationships, and become effective collaborators in achieving our goals.

Managing emotions during challenges and setbacks is another vital aspect of personal development. Life is full of ups and downs, and it is natural to experience a range of emotions throughout our journey. By learning to navigate through difficult emotions, such as disappointment or failure, we can bounce back stronger, stay focused on our goals, and persevere in the face of adversity.

In conclusion, understanding emotions and their impact is a fundamental aspect of personal development. By gaining insight into our emotions, managing them effectively, and harnessing their power, we can steer our destiny towards success. Emotions can either propel us forward or hold us back; it is up to us to master them and use them as a tool for achieving our goals.

Managing and Regulating Emotions

Emotions play a crucial role in our lives, impacting our thoughts, behaviors, and overall well-being. However, without proper management and regulation, emotions can become overwhelming and hinder our personal development goals. In this subchapter, we will explore effective strategies to help you master your emotions and achieve your desired outcomes.

The first step in managing and regulating emotions is to develop self-awareness. Understanding and recognizing your emotions is essential for effectively dealing with them. Take the time to identify the emotions you are experiencing and explore the underlying causes. This self-reflection will empower you to address your emotions more constructively.

Once you have identified your emotions, it is crucial to learn how to regulate them. One effective technique is deep breathing. Take slow, deep breaths to calm your body and mind. This simple practice helps activate the relaxation response and reduces the intensity of negative emotions.

Another powerful tool for managing emotions is reframing. Reframing involves consciously changing the way you perceive a situation. Instead of dwelling on the negative aspects, focus on finding the positive or learning opportunities. Shifting your perspective can lead to a more balanced emotional state and provide a clearer path towards achieving your goals.

It is also beneficial to develop healthy coping mechanisms for dealing with intense emotions. Engaging in physical activities such as exercise or engaging in hobbies that bring you joy can help release negative energy. Additionally, seeking support from friends, family, or a therapist can provide valuable guidance and perspective during challenging times.

Furthermore, mindfulness practices can greatly assist in managing and regulating emotions. Mindfulness involves bringing your attention to the present moment without judgment. By practicing mindfulness, you can cultivate a greater sense of self-control and respond to emotions in a more thoughtful and deliberate manner.

Remember, managing and regulating emotions is an ongoing process. It requires consistent effort and practice. By implementing these strategies and techniques, you can develop a greater understanding of your emotions and use them as a powerful tool to propel you towards your personal development goals.

In conclusion, emotions are an integral part of our lives, but they need to be managed and regulated to ensure personal growth and development. Developing self-awareness, regulating emotions through deep breathing and reframing, adopting healthy coping mechanisms, seeking support, and practicing mindfulness are all effective strategies to help you master your emotions and achieve your desired outcomes. By actively managing and regulating your emotions, you can create a positive and fulfilling life, aligning with your personal development goals.

Building Empathy and Compassion

In our journey towards personal development, one of the most important goals we can set for ourselves is to build empathy and compassion. These two qualities are essential in creating meaningful relationships, fostering understanding, and making a positive impact on the world around us. Regardless of our background, interests, or aspirations, developing empathy and compassion can benefit every one of us.

Empathy is the ability to understand and share the feelings of another person. It allows us to put ourselves in someone else's shoes and truly comprehend their emotions and experiences. By actively practicing empathy, we become more attuned to the needs of others and can respond with kindness and understanding. This not only strengthens our relationships but also helps create a more inclusive and compassionate society.

Compassion, on the other hand, takes empathy a step further by inspiring action. When we feel compassion towards someone, we are motivated to help alleviate their suffering or support them in their challenges. Compassion is not just a feeling; it is the driving force behind acts of kindness, generosity, and service. By cultivating compassion, we become agents of positive change and make a tangible difference in the lives of others.

So, how can we build empathy and compassion in our lives? It starts with self-reflection and a genuine desire to understand and connect with others. We can actively listen to people's stories, perspectives, and struggles, without judgment or preconceived notions. By practicing non-judgmental listening, we create safe spaces for others to express themselves authentically.

Additionally, we can educate ourselves about different cultures, beliefs, and experiences. By expanding our knowledge and challenging our own biases, we become more open-minded and accepting of diversity. This, in turn, fosters empathy and compassion towards those who may have different backgrounds or life experiences than our own.

Furthermore, acts of kindness and service play a crucial role in building empathy and compassion. Simple gestures like offering a helping hand, volunteering, or engaging in random acts of kindness can have a profound impact on both the giver and the receiver. These acts remind us of our interconnectedness and reinforce our sense of empathy and compassion.

In conclusion, building empathy and compassion is a universal goal that can benefit every one of us. By developing these qualities, we enhance our relationships, contribute to a more compassionate society, and find fulfillment in making a positive difference. Let us embrace empathy and compassion, for they hold the power to transform our lives and shape a better future for all.

Improving Communication and Relationship Skills

In today's fast-paced world, effective communication and healthy relationships are more important than ever. Whether you are striving to achieve personal or professional goals, mastering the art of communication and building strong relationships is essential for success. In this subchapter, we explore various strategies and techniques to help you improve your communication skills and foster positive relationships with others.

Communication is the foundation of all human interactions. It affects every aspect of our lives, from our personal relationships to our careers. By enhancing your communication skills, you can express yourself more clearly, understand others better, and resolve conflicts more effectively. We delve into the importance of active listening, nonverbal communication, and assertiveness techniques that can greatly enhance your ability to communicate with others.

Moreover, building strong relationships is vital in achieving your goals. Whether it's collaborating with colleagues, networking with professionals, or nurturing personal connections, maintaining healthy relationships is key. We provide strategies for effective networking, conflict resolution, and building trust, which are crucial for fostering meaningful connections and achieving your objectives.

Additionally, we explore the impact of emotional intelligence on communication and relationships. Emotional intelligence is the ability to recognize and manage your own emotions as well as understand and empathize with others. By developing emotional intelligence, you can navigate interpersonal dynamics with ease, cultivate empathy, and build stronger connections.

Furthermore, we discuss the role of effective communication and relationship skills in personal and professional growth. We provide practical tips for giving constructive feedback, managing difficult conversations, and setting boundaries to ensure healthy relationships. These skills are not only essential for achieving your goals but also for maintaining your overall well-being.

Whether you are an aspiring professional, a student, or simply someone seeking personal development, improving communication and relationship skills is vital. By mastering these skills, you can enhance your ability to connect with others, resolve conflicts, and achieve your goals with greater ease.

In conclusion, effective communication and healthy relationships are essential for personal and professional growth. By improving your communication skills and building strong relationships, you can enhance your ability to connect with others, achieve your goals, and lead a fulfilling life. This subchapter provides valuable insights, techniques, and strategies to help you master the art of communication and relationship building. So, take the first step towards improving your communication and relationship skills, and unlock your true potential!

Chapter 4: Enhancing Self-Discipline and Motivation

Defining Self-Discipline and Its Benefits

Self-discipline is the cornerstone of personal development and the key to achieving your goals. It is the ability to control your impulses, emotions, and behaviors in order to stay focused on what truly matters. In essence, it is about making conscious choices that align with your long-term objectives, even when faced with distractions or temptations. Mastering self-discipline is a skill that anyone can cultivate, regardless of their background or circumstances.

Self-discipline brings about numerous benefits that can transform your life. Firstly, it allows you to take control of your actions and make deliberate choices. Instead of being driven by momentary desires or external influences, self-discipline empowers you to act in accordance with your values and aspirations. This leads to a sense of personal fulfillment and a stronger sense of identity.

Furthermore, self-discipline breeds consistency and perseverance. By developing the ability to stick to your goals and follow through on your commitments, you increase your chances of success. Whether you are striving for career advancement, improving your health, or enhancing your relationships, self-discipline ensures that you consistently put in the necessary effort and remain committed, even in the face of challenges.

Self-discipline also enhances your productivity and time management skills. By prioritizing your tasks and staying focused, you become more efficient in utilizing your time and energy. With self-discipline, you can overcome procrastination and eliminate time-wasting activities, enabling you to accomplish more in less time.

Moreover, self-discipline fosters personal growth and continuous improvement. It encourages you to step out of your comfort zone and embrace new challenges, knowing that they are essential for growth. By pushing yourself to learn new skills and acquire knowledge, you expand your capabilities and become better equipped to tackle future endeavors.

In conclusion, self-discipline is a fundamental attribute that empowers individuals to achieve their goals and unlock their full potential. By cultivating self-discipline, you gain control over your actions, develop consistency, enhance productivity, and fuel personal growth. It is a lifelong journey of self-mastery that requires commitment, perseverance, and conscious decision-making. Regardless of your background or aspirations, mastering self-discipline is a transformative endeavor that can propel you towards the fulfillment of your dreams.

Overcoming Procrastination

Procrastination is a common obstacle that hinders many individuals from achieving their goals. Whether it's putting off starting a new project, postponing important tasks, or delaying personal growth, the habit of procrastination can have a significant impact on our lives. However, by understanding the root causes of procrastination and implementing effective strategies, we can overcome this habit and move closer to mastering our destiny.

One of the primary reasons for procrastination is fear. Fear of failure, fear of success, or even fear of the unknown can paralyze us and prevent us from taking action. It's crucial to identify and acknowledge these fears, as they often lie beneath our procrastination tendencies. By addressing and challenging these fears, we can gain the courage to move forward.

Another factor contributing to procrastination is the lack of clarity and focus. When we are unsure about our goals and lack a clear plan of action, it becomes easier to postpone tasks. To overcome this, it is essential to set specific, measurable, achievable, relevant, and time-bound (SMART) goals. Breaking down these goals into smaller, manageable tasks can help us stay focused and motivated.

Moreover, external distractions play a significant role in procrastination. With the constant availability of social media, entertainment, and other distractions, it is easy to lose track of time and prioritize immediate gratification over long-term goals. Establishing healthy boundaries and creating a conducive environment for productivity can help combat these distractions.

Procrastination can also stem from a lack of self-discipline and poor time management skills. By developing a structured schedule, setting priorities, and practicing self-discipline, we can overcome the temptation to procrastinate and make consistent progress towards our goals.

Accountability is another powerful tool in overcoming procrastination. Sharing our goals with others and seeking their support and feedback can help keep us on track. Additionally, finding an accountability partner or joining a mastermind group can provide the necessary motivation and encouragement to overcome our procrastination tendencies.

Overcoming procrastination is a journey that requires self-reflection, commitment, and perseverance. By understanding the underlying causes, setting clear goals, managing distractions, improving time management, and seeking accountability, we can break free from the habit of procrastination and take charge of our destiny.

Remember, every one of us has the potential to overcome procrastination and achieve our personal development goals. It all starts with making a conscious decision to take action today and commit to the pursuit of our dreams.

Setting and Achieving SMART Goals

In today's fast-paced and ever-changing world, setting and achieving goals is crucial for personal development and growth. Whether you are a student, a professional, or a stay-at-home parent, having clear and attainable goals can provide a sense of direction and purpose in life. This subchapter will introduce you to the concept of SMART goals and how to effectively set and achieve them.

SMART goals are Specific, Measurable, Attainable, Relevant, and Time-bound. Each of these components plays a vital role in ensuring that your goals are well-defined and realistic. By following these principles, you can increase your chances of success and stay motivated throughout your journey.

First and foremost, your goals should be specific. Instead of setting vague objectives like "lose weight" or "save money," be precise about what you want to achieve. For example, you could aim to lose 10 pounds in three months or save $500 by the end of the year. By making your goals specific, you can focus your efforts and create a clear roadmap to follow.

Secondly, your goals should be measurable. This means that you should include tangible criteria to track your progress. For instance, if your goal is to read more books, specify a number such as "read one book per month." This way, you can easily monitor your progress and make adjustments if needed.

Next, ensure that your goals are attainable. While it's important to challenge yourself, setting unrealistic goals can lead to frustration and disappointment. Consider your current resources, skills, and time commitments when determining what is achievable for you. By setting attainable goals, you will feel more empowered and motivated to work towards them.

Additionally, your goals should be relevant to your overall aspirations and values. They should align with your long-term vision and contribute to your personal growth. Setting goals that are meaningful to you will increase your dedication and enthusiasm to achieve them.

Lastly, make your goals time-bound by setting deadlines. Without a timeframe, goals can easily be put on the back burner. Setting a specific date or timeframe creates a sense of urgency and helps you stay accountable to yourself.

Remember, setting and achieving SMART goals is a continuous process. Regularly review and revise your goals as you progress and as your priorities shift. By adopting the SMART approach to goal setting, you can master your destiny and unlock your full potential.

So, take a moment to reflect on your aspirations, and start setting SMART goals today. With dedication, perseverance, and the right mindset, you can achieve anything you set your mind to. Don't wait for tomorrow; start shaping your future today.

Finding and Maintaining Motivation

Motivation is the driving force that propels us towards our goals. It is the fire that keeps us going when faced with challenges and obstacles. Without motivation, it is easy to lose sight of our objectives and settle for mediocrity. In this subchapter, we will delve into the art of finding and maintaining motivation, offering practical tips and strategies for individuals from all walks of life.

One of the first steps to finding motivation is identifying your goals. What is it that you truly want to achieve? Take some time to reflect on your aspirations, both short-term and long-term. Write them down and visualize what your life would look like once you accomplish them. This exercise will help you connect with your deepest desires and ignite the passion within you.

However, simply identifying your goals is not enough. To maintain motivation, it is crucial to break them down into smaller, manageable tasks. Setting achievable milestones will give you a sense of progress and keep you motivated along the way. Celebrate each small victory, as it will fuel your determination to continue moving forward.

Another secret to staying motivated is to surround yourself with positive influences. Seek out individuals who share similar goals or have achieved what you aspire to accomplish. Their success stories and guidance can be a source of inspiration during challenging times. Additionally, eliminate negative influences that drain your motivation and energy. Surround yourself with positive affirmations, inspirational quotes, and uplifting music to create an environment that fuels motivation.

It is important to remember that motivation is not constant. There will be moments when you feel demotivated or face setbacks. During these times, it is essential to practice self-compassion and focus on self-care. Take breaks, engage in activities that bring you joy, and remember that setbacks are a part of the journey towards success. Use these moments as opportunities to learn and grow, and then get back on track with renewed determination.

In conclusion, finding and maintaining motivation is a lifelong journey. By identifying your goals, breaking them down into actionable steps, surrounding yourself with positive influences, and practicing self-care during challenging times, you can fuel your motivation and propel yourself towards success. Remember, motivation is not something you find once and keep forever; it requires continuous effort and adaptation. Mastering the art of motivation will enable you to conquer any obstacle and achieve your personal development goals.

Chapter 5: Time Management and Productivity

Assessing Your Time Management Skills

Time is a precious resource that we all have in equal measure. Yet, it often seems like there is never enough time to accomplish all that we want to do. The key to overcoming this challenge lies in mastering our time management skills. In this subchapter, we will explore how to assess your time management skills and identify areas for improvement.

Assessing your time management skills is the first step towards effective goal-setting and personal development. It allows you to gain a clear understanding of how you currently manage your time and determine if any changes are necessary. To begin, take a moment to reflect on your daily routine. Are you often overwhelmed by tasks? Do you find yourself frequently procrastinating? Are you easily distracted or struggle to prioritize your activities? These are all signs that your time management skills may need improvement.

One useful tool in assessing your time management skills is keeping a time log. This involves recording how you spend your time throughout the day for at least a week. Be honest and detailed in your entries, noting the specific activities you engage in and how much time you allocate to each. This exercise will provide you with a visual representation of how you currently manage your time and help you identify patterns or areas of concern.

Once you have a clear picture of your time management habits, it is important to evaluate your goals and priorities. Ask yourself: Are the tasks I am spending my time on aligned with my long-term goals? Are there any activities that are not contributing to my personal development? This self-reflection will enable you to determine if you are allocating your time in a way that supports your overall objectives.

Furthermore, it is essential to identify any time-wasting activities or distractions that hinder your productivity. These could include excessive social media use, aimless web browsing, or spending too much time on unproductive conversations. By recognizing these time thieves, you can take steps to minimize or eliminate them from your daily routine, allowing you to focus on high-priority tasks.

In conclusion, assessing your time management skills is crucial for personal development and goal achievement. By keeping a time log, evaluating your goals, and identifying time-wasting activities, you can gain valuable insights into how you currently manage your time and make necessary adjustments. Remember, effective time management is a skill that can be developed and mastered with practice. So, take control of your time, and you will be well on your way to mastering your destiny.

Prioritizing Tasks and Setting Deadlines

In the fast-paced world we live in, it's easy to feel overwhelmed by the sheer number of tasks and responsibilities demanding our attention. Whether it's at work, school, or in our personal lives, mastering the art of prioritizing tasks and setting deadlines is crucial for achieving our goals and ultimately taking control of our destiny.

Prioritizing tasks involves determining which tasks are most important and need to be completed first. This requires a clear understanding of our goals and objectives. By aligning our tasks with our overarching goals, we can ensure that our efforts are focused on what truly matters.

One effective method for prioritizing tasks is using the Eisenhower Matrix, which categorizes tasks into four quadrants based on their urgency and importance. The first quadrant includes tasks that are both urgent and important, such as deadlines or critical tasks that cannot be delayed. These should be given top priority. The second quadrant consists of important but not urgent tasks, which should be scheduled and allocated time for completion. The third quadrant includes urgent but less important tasks, which can often be delegated or minimized. The fourth and final quadrant comprises tasks that are neither urgent nor important, and these should be eliminated or postponed if possible.

Once we have prioritized our tasks, it is essential to set deadlines for each one. Deadlines provide a sense of urgency and help us stay focused and motivated. When setting deadlines, it's important to be realistic and consider factors such as the complexity of the task and our available resources. Breaking larger tasks into smaller, manageable subtasks with their own deadlines can also help prevent overwhelm and increase productivity.

To effectively prioritize tasks and meet deadlines, it's crucial to manage our time efficiently. This involves eliminating distractions, creating a schedule or to-do list, and developing good time management habits. By allocating specific time blocks for each task and setting aside time for breaks and self-care, we can optimize our productivity and ensure that our tasks are completed within the designated deadlines.

In conclusion, mastering the art of prioritizing tasks and setting deadlines is vital for achieving our personal development goals. By aligning our tasks with our overarching goals, utilizing effective prioritization techniques, and managing our time efficiently, we can take control of our destiny and make significant progress towards our aspirations. Remember, every one of us can benefit from prioritizing tasks and setting deadlines – no matter our background or niche.

Effective Planning and Organization Techniques

In today's fast-paced world, where time seems to fly by and demands on our lives are constantly increasing, it is essential to have effective planning and organization techniques in place. Whether you are a student, a professional, or a stay-at-home parent, mastering these skills can significantly enhance your ability to achieve your goals and lead a productive and fulfilling life.

One of the key aspects of effective planning is setting clear and specific goals. Without a destination in mind, it becomes challenging to create a roadmap to success. Whether your goals are related to your career, personal life, or health, clearly defining what you want to achieve allows you to focus your efforts and channel your energy towards the desired outcomes.

Once you have established your goals, breaking them down into smaller, manageable tasks is crucial. This technique not only helps to prevent overwhelm but also provides a sense of accomplishment as you tick off each completed task. By breaking down your goals into smaller steps, you can easily track your progress and make adjustments along the way.

To ensure successful completion of your tasks, it is vital to prioritize them. Identify which tasks are the most important and urgent, and allocate your time and resources accordingly. By focusing on high-priority tasks, you can avoid unnecessary distractions and make the most of your available time.

Another valuable technique is creating a schedule or a to-do list. This allows you to allocate specific time slots for different tasks and helps you stay organized and on track. It is important to be realistic when planning your schedule, considering factors such as your energy levels and potential unforeseen circumstances.

In addition to planning and scheduling, effective organization is crucial for success. Keep your workspace tidy and clutter-free, as a chaotic environment can hinder productivity and increase stress levels. Develop systems for organizing your documents, emails, and other essential items, so you can easily access them when needed.

Lastly, don't forget to build in time for self-care and relaxation. Taking breaks and allowing yourself moments of rest is vital for maintaining focus and preventing burnout. Remember, effective planning and organization is not about working harder, but about working smarter.

In conclusion, mastering effective planning and organization techniques is vital for achieving your goals and leading a fulfilling life. By setting clear goals, breaking them down into manageable tasks, prioritizing, scheduling, and maintaining an organized environment, you can enhance your productivity, reduce stress, and ultimately take control of your destiny.

Overcoming Time Wasters and Distractions

In today's fast-paced world, time has become one of the most valuable commodities. We often find ourselves struggling to manage our time effectively, as various distractions and time wasters constantly vie for our attention. However, if we wish to achieve our personal development goals, it is imperative that we learn to overcome these obstacles and take control of our time.

The first step in overcoming time wasters and distractions is to identify them. Take a moment to reflect on the activities that consume a significant portion of your time without contributing to your personal growth or productivity. It could be excessive social media usage, watching too much television, or even constantly checking your phone for notifications. Once you have identified these time wasters, make a conscious effort to limit or eliminate them from your daily routine.

Another effective strategy is to create a schedule or a to-do list. By planning your day in advance, you can allocate specific time slots for important tasks and minimize the risk of getting sidetracked. Prioritize your goals and allocate dedicated time for working towards them. This will help you stay focused and make progress in achieving your personal development goals.

In order to overcome distractions, it is crucial to create an environment conducive to productivity. Find a quiet and organized space where you can work without interruptions. Turn off notifications on your phone or use apps that block distracting websites during your dedicated work time. By creating boundaries and eliminating potential distractions, you can enhance your concentration and productivity.

Furthermore, practicing mindfulness can be immensely helpful in overcoming time wasters and distractions. Train your mind to stay present and fully engage in the task at hand. Whenever you feel the urge to indulge in a time-wasting activity or get distracted, take a deep breath and remind yourself of your goals. By consciously redirecting your focus, you can regain control over your time and make progress towards your personal development objectives.

In conclusion, mastering your destiny requires overcoming time wasters and distractions. By identifying and eliminating non-productive activities, creating a schedule, setting boundaries, and practicing mindfulness, you can take control of your time and propel yourself towards your personal development goals. Remember, time is a finite resource, and it is up to you to make the most of it. Start today and reclaim your time to create a brighter future for yourself.

Chapter 6: Cultivating Healthy Habits

Importance of Physical Health in Personal Development

In the pursuit of personal development and achieving our goals, it is essential to recognize the significant role that physical health plays in our overall well-being. Our physical health forms the foundation upon which we build our lives, enabling us to thrive in all areas of our personal development journey. This subchapter aims to highlight the importance of physical health and its direct impact on our personal growth and goal attainment.

Physical health encompasses various aspects, including exercise, nutrition, sleep, and overall self-care. Engaging in regular physical activity not only improves our physical fitness but also boosts our mental and emotional well-being. Exercise releases endorphins, the feel-good hormones that reduce stress, anxiety, and depression. By incorporating exercise into our daily routines, we can enhance our focus, productivity, and overall happiness, which are crucial factors in achieving our personal development goals.

Furthermore, proper nutrition is essential for sustaining energy levels, mental clarity, and overall vitality. A well-balanced diet provides the necessary nutrients to support our cognitive functions and maintain optimal physical health. By fueling our bodies with nutritious foods, we can enhance our brainpower, improve our mood, and increase our resilience in the face of challenges.

Another crucial aspect of physical health is adequate sleep. Quality sleep is vital for our physical and mental restoration. It allows our bodies to recover from daily exertions, repair damaged tissues, and consolidate memories. Getting enough sleep ensures that we wake up refreshed and ready to tackle the day, enabling us to stay focused on our personal development goals.

Lastly, practicing self-care is essential for maintaining physical health. It involves activities such as relaxation, stress management, and engaging in activities that bring us joy and fulfillment. Taking time for ourselves not only rejuvenates our bodies but also nourishes our souls, allowing us to approach our personal development journey with renewed vigor and enthusiasm.

In conclusion, physical health forms an integral part of personal development goals for everyone. By prioritizing our physical well-being through regular exercise, proper nutrition, sufficient sleep, and self-care, we lay a strong foundation for personal growth and goal attainment. When our bodies are healthy and strong, our minds become sharper, and our spirits soar higher. Let us embrace the importance of physical health on our personal development journey and unlock our true potential to master our destiny.

Creating a Balanced Diet and Exercise Routine

In our fast-paced world, it can be challenging to find the time and motivation to prioritize our health. However, establishing a balanced diet and exercise routine is crucial for achieving personal development goals. Whether your goal is to lose weight, increase energy levels, or improve overall well-being, incorporating healthy eating and regular physical activity into your lifestyle is essential.

A balanced diet is the foundation of good health. It involves consuming a variety of nutrients that nourish your body and support its optimal functioning. To achieve this, aim to include foods from all major food groups in your meals. This includes fruits, vegetables, whole grains, lean proteins, and healthy fats. Strive to limit processed foods, sugary snacks, and excessive salt or saturated fats. Remember, moderation is key.

In addition to a balanced diet, regular exercise is equally important. Engaging in physical activity not only helps maintain a healthy weight but also improves cardiovascular health, enhances mood, and boosts energy levels. Find an exercise routine that suits your preferences and lifestyle. It could be anything from brisk walking, jogging, swimming, yoga, or joining a fitness class. The key is to be consistent and make it a habit. Start with small goals and gradually increase the intensity and duration of your workouts.

To make your fitness journey more enjoyable, consider finding a workout buddy or joining a local sports team or gym. Surrounding yourself with like-minded individuals can provide motivation, support, and accountability. Set realistic goals and track your progress to stay motivated. Celebrate even the small achievements along the way.

Remember that creating a balanced diet and exercise routine is not about depriving yourself or pushing your body to extremes. It's about finding a healthy balance that suits your individual needs and preferences. Listen to your body, be mindful of your food choices, and find joy in being active.

Lastly, it's important to consult with a healthcare professional or a registered dietitian before making any significant changes to your diet or exercise routine. They can provide personalized guidance and ensure that you're on the right track.

By adopting a balanced diet and exercise routine, you are taking a significant step towards mastering your destiny. Investing in your health will not only benefit you physically but also mentally and emotionally. So, start today and prioritize your well-being. You deserve it!

Getting Adequate Sleep and Rest

In our fast-paced and demanding world, it is not uncommon for sleep and rest to take a backseat to our ever-growing list of goals and responsibilities. However, neglecting our sleep and rest can have serious consequences on our overall well-being and hinder our ability to achieve our goals. In this subchapter, we will explore the importance of getting adequate sleep and rest and how it contributes to our personal development goals.

Sleep is not a luxury; it is a necessity for optimal functioning. When we sleep, our bodies and minds have the chance to reset and recharge, allowing us to wake up feeling refreshed and ready to tackle the day ahead. Adequate sleep has numerous benefits, including improved cognitive function, increased productivity, enhanced creativity, and a strengthened immune system. Without enough sleep, we may experience difficulties concentrating, making decisions, and managing our emotions, all of which can hinder our progress towards our goals.

Rest, on the other hand, goes beyond sleep and encompasses activities that help us relax and rejuvenate. Engaging in restful activities such as meditation, deep breathing exercises, or pursuing hobbies we enjoy, allows our minds to unwind and recharge. Resting not only helps us manage stress but also enhances our ability to focus, problem-solve, and think creatively. By incorporating regular rest into our daily routines, we can improve our overall well-being and increase our chances of achieving our personal development goals.

So how can we ensure we are getting adequate sleep and rest? First and foremost, it is essential to prioritize sleep and rest in our daily schedules. Set a consistent sleep schedule, aiming for at least 7-9 hours of sleep each night. Create a relaxing bedtime routine, such as reading a book or taking a warm bath, to signal to your body that it's time to wind down. Additionally, make an effort to incorporate restful activities into your day, even if it's just for a few minutes. Schedule breaks throughout your workday to stretch, breathe, or engage in a calming activity.

Remember, getting adequate sleep and rest is not a luxury but a crucial component of achieving your personal development goals. By prioritizing sleep and rest, you are investing in your overall well-being and setting yourself up for success. So, make a commitment to yourself today and start implementing healthy sleep and rest habits. Your body, mind, and goals will thank you.

Incorporating Relaxation and Stress-Management Techniques

In our fast-paced and demanding world, it is crucial to prioritize self-care and find effective ways to manage stress. Incorporating relaxation and stress-management techniques into our daily lives can greatly contribute to our overall well-being and help us achieve our personal development goals.

Stress, if left unaddressed, can have detrimental effects on both our physical and mental health. It can hinder our ability to focus, make sound decisions, and hinder our overall productivity. Therefore, it is essential for everyone, regardless of their goals, to incorporate relaxation techniques into their daily routine.

One of the most effective stress-management techniques is mindfulness meditation. By practicing mindfulness, we bring our attention to the present moment, allowing us to let go of worries about the future or regrets about the past. Regular practice of mindfulness meditation has been scientifically proven to reduce stress levels, improve focus, and enhance overall well-being.

Another powerful technique for stress management is deep breathing exercises. Deep breathing activates the body's relaxation response, helping to calm the mind and reduce stress. By taking slow, deep breaths and focusing on the sensation of the breath filling our lungs, we can instantly feel a sense of calmness and relaxation.

Physical activity is also an excellent way to manage stress and achieve personal development goals. Engaging in regular exercise not only improves our physical health but also releases endorphins, the "feel-good" hormones, which help reduce stress and boost our mood.

Whether it's going for a walk, practicing yoga, or participating in team sports, finding an activity that you enjoy and incorporating it into your routine can significantly contribute to your overall well-being.

Additionally, finding time for hobbies and activities that bring joy and relaxation can also be highly beneficial. Whether it's reading, painting, gardening, or listening to music, engaging in activities that allow you to disconnect from your daily stresses can provide a much-needed break and recharge your mind and body.

Incorporating relaxation and stress-management techniques into your life is not a luxury; it is a necessity. By taking care of your well-being and managing stress effectively, you will be better equipped to achieve your personal development goals. Prioritizing self-care and dedicating time to relaxation will not only improve your overall quality of life but also enhance your ability to navigate challenges and reach your fullest potential. Remember, your well-being is the foundation upon which your goals are built.

Chapter 7: Building Resilience and Overcoming Challenges

Understanding Resilience and Its Benefits

Resilience is a fundamental trait that empowers individuals to overcome obstacles, adapt to changes, and bounce back from adversity. In the journey of mastering your destiny and achieving personal development goals, resilience plays a pivotal role. It is an essential quality that can propel you forward, even in the face of challenges and setbacks. Regardless of your background or aspirations, understanding resilience and harnessing its benefits can significantly enhance your ability to achieve your goals.

Resilience can be defined as the ability to withstand and recover from difficult situations, whether they are personal or professional. It is not about avoiding or denying hardships; rather, it is about cultivating the strength to confront them head-on and emerge stronger than before. Resilient individuals possess an unwavering belief in their abilities and a positive mindset that enables them to view setbacks as opportunities for growth and learning.

One of the key benefits of resilience is the ability to adapt to change. In today's fast-paced world, where change is constant, being able to embrace and navigate it is vital for personal growth and success. Resilient individuals are flexible and open-minded, enabling them to adjust their plans and strategies when necessary. They see change as a chance to explore new possibilities and seize opportunities that may have otherwise been overlooked.

Moreover, resilience is closely linked to mental and emotional well-being. It helps individuals develop coping mechanisms and manage stress effectively. When faced with challenges, resilient individuals are more likely to maintain a positive outlook, which not only reduces anxiety but also enhances problem-solving abilities. By cultivating resilience, you can build a solid foundation for your mental health and overall well-being.

Resilience also fosters persistence and determination. It fuels the motivation to keep moving forward, even when the path seems uncertain or daunting. It enables individuals to stay committed to their goals, despite setbacks or failures along the way. By bouncing back from adversity, resilient individuals develop a sense of self-efficacy, knowing that they have the power to overcome any hurdle that comes their way.

In conclusion, understanding resilience and harnessing its benefits is crucial for anyone seeking personal development goals. Resilience empowers individuals to adapt to change, maintain mental and emotional well-being, and persist in the face of challenges. By cultivating resilience, you can unlock your full potential and master your destiny. So, embrace resilience as a guiding principle in your journey towards personal growth and success.

Developing a Growth Mindset

In the pursuit of personal development goals, one of the most valuable mindsets to cultivate is a growth mindset. This mindset not only allows you to embrace challenges and setbacks but also enables you to continuously learn, evolve, and ultimately reach your goals. Whether you are an entrepreneur, student, professional, or someone simply seeking self-improvement, developing a growth mindset can be the key to unlocking your true potential.

A growth mindset is the belief that abilities, intelligence, and talents can be developed through dedication, perseverance, and hard work. It is the understanding that failure is not a permanent state but rather an opportunity for learning and growth. With a growth mindset, you can approach challenges as stepping stones to success rather than insurmountable obstacles.

To develop a growth mindset, it is important to first recognize and challenge any fixed mindset beliefs you may hold. Fixed mindset beliefs are the assumptions that talents and abilities are fixed traits and cannot be changed. By acknowledging and challenging these beliefs, you open yourself up to the possibility of growth and improvement.

Embracing challenges is another crucial aspect of developing a growth mindset. Instead of avoiding difficult tasks, seek them out as opportunities to learn and grow. View failures not as indicators of your limitations but as valuable lessons that can propel you forward. By adopting this mindset, you will become more resilient and adaptable in the face of adversity.

Effort and perseverance are essential in developing a growth mindset. Understand that mastery and success require consistent effort and a willingness to put in the work. Embrace the process of learning and value the journey rather than focusing solely on the end result. Celebrate small victories and use setbacks as fuel to propel you forward.

Another important element of developing a growth mindset is seeking out feedback and learning from others. Surround yourself with individuals who encourage and challenge you to grow. Embrace constructive criticism as an opportunity for improvement rather than taking it personally.

In conclusion, developing a growth mindset is crucial for anyone looking to achieve their personal development goals. By embracing challenges, persisting through setbacks, and valuing effort and feedback, you can unlock your true potential and become the master of your own destiny. Remember, success is not limited to a select few but is attainable by anyone willing to cultivate a growth mindset.

Embracing Change and Adaptability

In the fast-paced world we live in today, change is inevitable. It is a constant in our lives, whether we like it or not. In order to succeed and achieve our personal development goals, we must learn to embrace change and become adaptable individuals.

Change can be intimidating and even frightening for many people. We often find ourselves resisting it, clinging to our comfort zones and routines. However, change is not something to be feared, but rather something to be embraced. It is through change that we grow and evolve as individuals.

To master your destiny and achieve your goals, you must be willing to step out of your comfort zone and embrace the unknown. This requires a mindset shift – a willingness to let go of old patterns and beliefs that no longer serve you. When faced with change, instead of resisting it, ask yourself, "How can I adapt and make the most of this situation?"

Adaptability is a key trait of successful individuals. Those who are adaptable are able to navigate through life's challenges with ease and grace. They are able to quickly adjust their plans, strategies, and mindset in response to changing circumstances. This flexibility allows them to seize new opportunities and overcome obstacles that come their way.

To become adaptable, it is important to cultivate a growth mindset. Believe in your ability to learn and grow from any situation. See challenges as opportunities for growth and view failures as stepping stones to success. Embrace a mindset of continuous learning and improvement, and you will become more resilient and adaptable.

Developing a strong support system is also crucial in embracing change and adaptability. Surround yourself with like-minded individuals who support your personal development goals. Seek out mentors and coaches who can guide you through the process of change. Connect with a community that shares your values and aspirations. Having a support system helps you stay accountable, motivated, and resilient in the face of change.

Remember, change is the only constant in life. By embracing change and becoming adaptable, you can master your destiny and achieve your personal development goals. Embrace the unknown, cultivate a growth mindset, and build a strong support system. You have the power to embrace change and adapt to any circumstances that come your way. Embrace change, and you will unlock your full potential.

Strategies for Overcoming Obstacles and Setbacks

Life is an unpredictable journey filled with both triumphs and challenges. Along the path towards achieving our goals, we are bound to encounter obstacles and setbacks. However, it is important to remember that these obstacles do not define us; rather, they present opportunities for growth and learning. In this subchapter, we will explore effective strategies for overcoming obstacles and setbacks, allowing you to master your destiny and reach your personal development goals.

1. Embrace a Positive Mindset: The first step towards conquering any obstacle is to cultivate a positive mindset. By maintaining a positive attitude, you can shift your perspective and view setbacks as temporary hurdles rather than insurmountable roadblocks. Embrace the belief that challenges are opportunities for personal growth and transformation.

2. Develop Resilience: Resilience is the key to bouncing back from setbacks. Cultivate resilience by developing a strong support system, practicing self-care, and nurturing your mental and emotional well-being. Surround yourself with positive influences, engage in activities that bring you joy, and prioritize self-care practices such as exercise, meditation, and gratitude.

3. Set Realistic Expectations: Often, setbacks arise when we set unrealistic expectations for ourselves. Ensure that your goals are achievable and realistic, breaking them down into smaller, manageable steps. By setting attainable milestones, you can celebrate small victories along the way, boosting your motivation and resilience.

4. Learn from Failure: Failure is not the end; it is an opportunity to learn and grow. Instead of dwelling on your mistakes, analyze them to identify valuable lessons. Reflect on what went wrong, adjust your approach accordingly, and use these experiences as stepping stones towards future success.

5. Seek Support: Facing obstacles alone can be daunting. Reach out to friends, family, or mentors who can provide guidance, encouragement, and support. Collaborate with like-minded individuals who share similar goals, as their experiences and insights can offer fresh perspectives and solutions.

6. Adapt and Innovate: When obstacles arise, be flexible and open to adapting your strategies. Embrace innovation by exploring alternative approaches and thinking outside the box. Sometimes, the most effective solutions emerge when we are willing to step outside our comfort zones and explore new possibilities.

Remember, setbacks are not indicators of failure, but rather opportunities for growth. By implementing these strategies and maintaining a positive mindset, you can overcome obstacles, achieve your goals, and master your destiny. Embrace challenges as stepping stones towards personal development, and watch as you transform setbacks into catalysts for success.

Chapter 8: Nurturing Relationships and Social Skills

Importance of Healthy Relationships for Personal Growth

In our journey towards personal growth and self-improvement, it is crucial to recognize the immense significance of healthy relationships. Whether it is with our family, friends, romantic partners, or even colleagues, cultivating and nurturing these connections can have a profound impact on our overall well-being and personal development. This subchapter delves into the importance of healthy relationships for personal growth, highlighting the essential role they play in our pursuit of goals and self-fulfillment.

Human beings are inherently social creatures, and our relationships form the foundation of our emotional and psychological well-being. Healthy relationships provide us with a sense of belonging, support, and companionship, all of which are vital for personal growth. When we surround ourselves with positive and supportive individuals, their influence can greatly impact our mindset, beliefs, and behaviors. They can serve as catalysts in our journey towards self-improvement and achieving our goals.

One of the key benefits of healthy relationships lies in the opportunity for personal growth through constructive feedback and accountability. By engaging with individuals who genuinely care about our well-being, we expose ourselves to valuable insights and perspectives. These relationships act as mirrors, reflecting our strengths and weaknesses, enabling us to identify areas for improvement and personal growth. Constructive criticism and feedback from trusted individuals can be transformative, helping us challenge our limiting beliefs and encouraging us to step outside our comfort zones.

Furthermore, healthy relationships foster personal growth by providing a safe space for self-expression and vulnerability. When we feel accepted and supported by others, we are more likely to embrace our authentic selves and take risks. This environment allows us to explore our passions, interests, and talents, which are crucial aspects of personal development. By sharing our dreams and aspirations with those we trust, we receive encouragement and motivation, propelling us towards our goals.

In conclusion, healthy relationships are indispensable for personal growth. They offer emotional support, constructive feedback, and a nurturing environment for self-expression. By surrounding ourselves with positive and supportive individuals, we enhance our chances of achieving our goals and unlocking our true potential. It is essential to recognize the value of these relationships and invest time and effort in nurturing them. By doing so, we open ourselves up to a world of personal growth and self-fulfillment.

Effective Communication and Active Listening

In the pursuit of personal development goals, one skill that holds paramount importance is effective communication. No matter who we are or what our goals may be, the ability to communicate effectively is essential in achieving success and fostering meaningful connections in both our personal and professional lives.

Communication is not simply about speaking; it is also about active listening. Active listening involves fully engaging with others, not just hearing their words, but also understanding their emotions, perspectives, and underlying messages. By actively listening to others, we can gain valuable insights, build trust, and forge strong relationships based on empathy and understanding.

In today's fast-paced world, where distractions are abundant, active listening has become a rare commodity. However, it is a skill that can be honed with practice and dedication. It requires us to set aside our own preconceived notions and judgments, and truly immerse ourselves in the speaker's world. By doing so, we not only demonstrate respect for the other person but also create an environment conducive to open and honest communication.

To become effective communicators, we must also be mindful of our own words and actions. It is crucial to choose our words carefully, ensuring they are clear, concise, and respectful. Communication is a two-way street, and active communication involves actively seeking feedback and responding appropriately. By practising open and honest communication, we can foster trust, resolve conflicts, and inspire others to share their thoughts and ideas.

In addition to verbal communication, non-verbal cues play a significant role in effective communication. Our body language, facial expressions, and tone of voice can convey more than words alone. Being aware of our non-verbal cues and understanding their impact can help us communicate more effectively and avoid misunderstandings.

Effective communication is an ongoing process that requires constant effort and self-reflection. It requires us to be present in the moment, listen attentively, and respond thoughtfully. By mastering the art of active listening and effective communication, we can enhance our relationships, improve our problem-solving abilities, and achieve our personal development goals.

Whether our goals revolve around career advancement, personal growth, or building meaningful connections, effective communication and active listening will undoubtedly play a pivotal role in our journey towards mastering our destiny. Let us embrace these skills, practice them diligently, and watch as our personal development goals come within reach.

Building and Maintaining Supportive Networks

In the journey of personal development, one crucial aspect that often gets overlooked is the power of building and maintaining supportive networks. Whether you are striving to achieve your goals in your personal or professional life, having a strong support system can make all the difference. This subchapter will delve into the importance of building these networks and provide practical tips on how to create and nurture them effectively.

Supportive networks serve as pillars of strength during challenging times and sources of inspiration throughout the pursuit of our goals. They provide a safe space for us to share our dreams, fears, and aspirations. These networks can consist of friends, family members, mentors, colleagues, or even online communities of like-minded individuals who understand and encourage us. They offer a platform for constructive feedback, guidance, and accountability, which are invaluable in our personal growth journey.

One of the first steps towards building a supportive network is identifying the people who align with your goals and values. Seek out individuals who share your passions, aspirations, or career interests. Engage in activities or join groups that align with your goals, as this will increase the chances of meeting like-minded individuals. Reach out and build genuine connections with these individuals, nurturing those relationships over time. Remember, quality is more important than quantity when it comes to building supportive networks.

Maintaining these networks requires consistent effort and genuine care. Show appreciation for the support you receive by reciprocating it whenever possible. Actively listen to others, show empathy, and provide support when they need it. Be mindful of being a positive influence and offering constructive feedback when necessary. Regularly check in with your network, even if it's just a quick message or a call. Celebrate each other's achievements and milestones, as this fosters a sense of belonging and motivates everyone to strive for their goals.

Building and maintaining supportive networks is not only beneficial for individual growth but also for the collective growth of the network. By surrounding ourselves with like-minded individuals who share our goals, we can create a community that lifts each other up and inspires one another to push boundaries and achieve greatness.

In conclusion, building and maintaining supportive networks is an essential component of personal development. These networks provide the necessary support, guidance, and accountability to help us reach our goals. By actively seeking out like-minded individuals, nurturing relationships, and showing genuine care, we can create a community that propels us towards our destiny. Remember, success is not a solitary journey, and together, we can achieve so much more.

Resolving Conflicts and Strengthening Connections

In the journey of personal development, conflicts are inevitable. Whether it's a disagreement with a loved one, a clash with a coworker, or an internal battle within ourselves, conflicts can hinder our progress towards achieving our goals. However, conflicts can also be opportunities for growth, learning, and strengthening connections with others. In this subchapter, we will explore effective strategies for resolving conflicts and building stronger relationships.

The first step in resolving conflicts is to adopt a mindset of understanding and empathy. It's important to recognize that everyone has their own perspectives, values, and experiences that shape their behavior. By seeking to understand the other person's point of view, we can approach conflicts with compassion and open-mindedness, fostering an environment of mutual respect.

Active listening is a powerful tool in conflict resolution. Often, conflicts arise from miscommunication or misunderstandings. By truly listening to the other person's thoughts and feelings, we can gain valuable insights into their needs and desires, enabling us to find common ground and work towards a resolution that satisfies both parties.

Managing emotions is another crucial aspect of conflict resolution. When conflicts arise, it's natural for emotions to run high. However, it's important to remain calm and composed, as reacting impulsively can escalate the situation. Taking deep breaths, practicing mindfulness, and using techniques such as "I" statements can help us express ourselves assertively without becoming defensive or aggressive.

Collaboration is key in resolving conflicts and strengthening connections. Instead of approaching conflicts as a win-lose situation, strive for win-win outcomes where both parties feel heard and their needs are met. This requires a willingness to compromise, find common interests, and explore creative solutions that address the root causes of the conflict.

Lastly, forgiveness and letting go are essential for personal growth and maintaining healthy relationships. Holding onto grudges or dwelling on past conflicts only hinders our progress. By practicing forgiveness, we can release negative emotions and move forward with a clean slate, fostering stronger connections with others.

In conclusion, conflicts are an inevitable part of life, but they also present opportunities for personal growth and stronger connections. By adopting a mindset of understanding, practicing active listening, managing emotions, collaborating, and embracing forgiveness, we can resolve conflicts in a way that supports our personal development goals. Remember, conflict resolution is not about winning or losing but rather about finding common ground, building empathy, and nurturing relationships. Let us embark on this journey of mastering our destiny by resolving conflicts and strengthening connections.

Chapter 9: Financial Management and Wealth Creation

Understanding the Role of Money in Personal Development

Money plays a crucial role in personal development. It is an essential tool that allows individuals to achieve their goals and fulfill their ambitions. While money should not be the sole focus of personal development, it is important to recognize its significance and understand how it can contribute to one's overall growth and well-being.

First and foremost, money provides individuals with the means to pursue their goals. Whether it is starting a business, furthering education, or investing in personal growth activities, financial resources are often required to make these aspirations a reality. Without money, many opportunities may remain out of reach, hindering personal development and limiting one's potential for growth.

Moreover, financial stability can significantly impact a person's mental and emotional well-being. Financial stress and uncertainty can be detrimental to personal growth, causing anxiety and hindering focus. By having a solid financial foundation, individuals can alleviate these concerns and concentrate on their personal development goals with a clear mind and an optimistic outlook.

Money can also provide individuals with the freedom to explore new avenues for personal growth. It allows for the pursuit of new experiences, such as traveling, attending workshops and seminars, or engaging in hobbies and interests. These experiences can broaden horizons, enhance skills, and foster personal development in various aspects of life.

However, it is essential to note that personal development should not solely revolve around accumulating wealth. Money is a means to an end, not the end itself. True personal development encompasses a holistic approach that includes physical, mental, emotional, and spiritual growth. It is about developing one's character, values, and relationships, in addition to financial well-being.

Therefore, individuals should approach money as a tool to support personal development rather than the sole measure of success. It is important to strike a balance between financial aspirations and overall well-being. This involves setting financial goals that align with personal values, practicing mindful spending and saving, and using money as a means to enhance personal growth rather than as a measure of self-worth.

In conclusion, money plays a crucial role in personal development by providing the means to pursue goals, alleviating financial stress, and enabling individuals to explore new avenues for growth. However, it is important to approach money as a tool rather than the sole measure of success. By balancing financial aspirations with overall well-being and personal growth, individuals can truly master their destiny and unlock their full potential.

Budgeting and Saving Strategies

Introduction:
In today's fast-paced and ever-changing world, it is crucial for everyone to have a solid grasp on budgeting and saving strategies. Whether you are a student, a young professional, a parent, or even nearing retirement, understanding how to manage your finances effectively can help you achieve your personal development goals. This subchapter aims to provide you with essential tips and strategies to master budgeting and saving, ensuring financial stability and a brighter future.

1. Set Financial Goals:
The first step in budgeting and saving is to define your financial goals. Whether it's saving for a dream vacation, buying a house, or creating an emergency fund, having clear objectives will help you stay motivated and focused on your financial journey.

2. Track Your Expenses:
Understanding where your money goes is crucial for effective budgeting. Start by tracking your expenses meticulously for a month. This will help you identify unnecessary spending habits and areas where you can cut back, leading to potential savings.

3. Create a Realistic Budget:
Once you have a clear picture of your expenses, it's time to create a budget. Allocate your income into different categories, such as housing, transportation, groceries, entertainment, and savings. Ensure that your expenses do not exceed your income, and prioritize saving a certain percentage of your earnings each month.

4.   Minimize   Debt:
High-interest debt can hinder your ability to save and achieve your goals. Develop a plan to pay off debts systematically, starting with those carrying the highest interest rates. Consider consolidating your debt or seeking professional advice to accelerate your debt repayment process.

5.   Automate   Savings:
Make saving a habit by automating it. Set up a direct deposit into a separate savings account or utilize an app that rounds up your purchases and saves the difference. By automating your savings, you eliminate the temptation to spend that money elsewhere.

6.   Cut   Back   on   Non-Essential   Expenses:
Evaluate your spending habits and identify areas where you can cut back without sacrificing your quality of life. Consider reducing dining out, entertainment subscriptions, or shopping for non-essential items. Small sacrifices in the present can lead to significant savings in the future.

7.   Review   and   Adjust:
Regularly review your budget and financial goals to ensure they align with your evolving circumstances. Life changes, such as career advancements or unexpected expenses, may require adjustments to your budget. Stay flexible and adapt your financial plan accordingly.

Conclusion:
Mastering budgeting and saving strategies is essential for everyone, regardless of their life stage or goals. By setting clear objectives, tracking expenses, creating a realistic budget, minimizing debt,

automating savings, and cutting back on non-essential expenses, you can take control of your financial destiny. Remember, small steps towards financial stability today can lead to a brighter and more prosperous future.

Investing and Growing Your Wealth

In today's fast-paced world, it's essential to have a solid plan for investing and growing your wealth. No matter who you are or what your goals may be, understanding the principles of smart investing can pave the way for financial success and allow you to achieve your personal development goals.

Investing is not just for the wealthy or the financially savvy; it's for everyone who wants to secure their future and build a legacy. Whether you're saving for retirement, planning to start a business, or simply aiming to increase your net worth, investing is the key to unlocking financial freedom.

The first step in investing is to educate yourself. Take the time to learn about different investment options, such as stocks, bonds, real estate, and mutual funds. Understand the risks and rewards associated with each investment vehicle, and choose the ones that align with your goals and risk tolerance.

Once you've gained a basic understanding of investing, it's time to set clear financial goals. What do you want to achieve? Do you want to retire early, buy a home, or travel the world? Define your goals and create a roadmap to reach them. Remember, investing is a long-term game, so be patient and stay focused on your objectives.

Diversification is another crucial aspect of investing. Spreading your investments across different asset classes and sectors can help mitigate risk and optimize returns. By diversifying your portfolio, you're not putting all your eggs in one basket and reducing the impact of any single investment's performance on your overall wealth.

Regularly reviewing and adjusting your investments is also essential. Keep track of market trends, economic indicators, and any changes in your personal circumstances that may require a reassessment of your investment strategy. Staying informed and proactive will help you make timely decisions and maximize your returns.

Lastly, seek professional advice when needed. Financial advisors can provide valuable insights and guidance tailored to your specific situation. They can help you create a personalized investment plan, monitor your progress, and make informed adjustments along the way.

Investing and growing your wealth is not an overnight process, but with dedication, discipline, and a clear plan, you can achieve your financial goals and pave the way for a brighter future. Start today, and take control of your destiny by mastering the art of investing.

Building Financial Security and Independence

In today's fast-paced and ever-changing world, achieving financial security and independence has become a top priority for individuals from all walks of life. Whether you are a recent graduate, a young professional, or someone nearing retirement, understanding and implementing strategies to build a solid financial foundation is crucial for a successful and fulfilling life.

This subchapter delves into the various aspects of building financial security and independence, providing practical tips and advice that can be applied by anyone, regardless of their current financial situation. By mastering the principles outlined in this chapter, you will be well on your way to achieving your personal development goals and securing a brighter future.

The first step towards building financial security is to set clear and achievable goals. By identifying your short-term and long-term objectives, you can create a roadmap that will guide your financial decisions and actions. Whether it's saving for a down payment on a house, paying off debt, or building an emergency fund, setting goals will give you a sense of purpose and direction.

Next, it is essential to establish a budget and stick to it. A budget helps you track your income and expenses, allowing you to make informed decisions about how you spend and save your money. By prioritizing your needs and cutting back on unnecessary expenses, you can free up funds to invest in your future and create a safety net for unexpected circumstances.

Another crucial aspect of building financial security is investing wisely. Educate yourself about various investment options such as stocks, bonds, real estate, and mutual funds. Diversify your portfolio to mitigate risks and maximize returns. Remember, investing is a long-term game, and patience and discipline are key to achieving financial independence.

Furthermore, it is important to protect yourself and your assets by having adequate insurance coverage. Health insurance, life insurance, and property insurance can provide peace of mind and safeguard you against unforeseen events that could jeopardize your financial stability.

Lastly, building a solid network of supportive individuals who share similar goals can greatly enhance your journey towards financial security and independence. Surround yourself with positive influences, seek advice from mentors, and learn from the experiences of others who have achieved financial success.

In conclusion, building financial security and independence is an ongoing process that requires dedication, discipline, and continuous learning. By setting clear goals, creating a budget, investing wisely, protecting yourself through insurance, and building a strong network, you can take control of your financial destiny and pave the way for a brighter and more prosperous future. Remember, the path to financial security begins with taking the first step. Start today and empower yourself to achieve your personal development goals.

Chapter 10: Creating a Meaningful Life and Legacy

Defining Your Life Purpose and Values

In the journey of personal development, understanding and defining your life purpose and values is crucial. It serves as a compass that guides your decisions, actions, and overall direction in life. Without a clear sense of purpose and values, you may find yourself feeling lost, unfulfilled, and unsure of what path to pursue. In this subchapter, we will delve into the process of discovering and defining your life purpose and values, empowering you to align your goals with your truest self.

First and foremost, it is important to understand that your life purpose is unique to you. It is not something that can be dictated by society, family, or friends. Your purpose is a reflection of your passions, talents, and the impact you wish to make in the world. To discover your purpose, take the time to reflect on what truly brings you joy and fulfillment. What activities or tasks make you lose track of time? What are the values that drive you? These questions will help you uncover the essence of your purpose.

Once you have a sense of your purpose, it's time to define your values. Your values are the principles and beliefs that guide your behavior and decision-making. They act as a moral compass, helping you navigate through life's challenges and opportunities. Identifying your values is a deeply personal process, and it requires a deep dive into your core beliefs. Consider the qualities you admire in others, the principles you hold dear, and the standards you strive to uphold.

With your purpose and values in mind, you can now align your goals to create a meaningful and purpose-driven life. Your goals should be an extension of your purpose and values, serving as stepping stones towards living a life that is in harmony with your true self. By setting goals that are in line with your purpose and values, you will find greater motivation, fulfillment, and a sense of direction.

Remember, mastering your destiny begins with understanding who you are and what truly matters to you. By defining your life purpose and values, you lay the foundation for personal growth and success. Embrace the journey of self-discovery and allow yourself the space and time to explore your passions, talents, and beliefs. With a clear sense of purpose and values, you will unlock your full potential and create a life that is truly your own.

Setting Meaningful Goals and Ambitions

In our journey towards personal growth and self-improvement, it is crucial to set meaningful goals and ambitions that align with our values and aspirations. Goals provide us with a sense of purpose, direction, and motivation. They give us something to strive for and help us measure our progress along the way. Whether you are a student, professional, or stay-at-home parent, setting meaningful goals can have a profound impact on your life.

To truly master your destiny, it is important to understand the significance of setting meaningful goals. The first step is to reflect on your values, passions, and long-term vision. What truly matters to you? What are your dreams and aspirations? Taking the time to introspect will help you identify goals that truly resonate with your inner self.

One key aspect of setting meaningful goals is ensuring that they are specific, measurable, achievable, relevant, and time-bound (SMART). By making your goals SMART, you create a clear roadmap for success. For example, instead of setting a vague goal like "I want to be successful," you can set a SMART goal like "I want to increase my annual income by 20% within the next two years by acquiring new skills and taking on additional responsibilities at work."

It is also important to break down your goals into smaller, manageable steps. This approach helps prevent overwhelm and allows you to track your progress more effectively. Celebrating small victories along the way will keep you motivated and focused on your ultimate goal.

Another crucial element of setting meaningful goals is ensuring they are realistic and aligned with your current circumstances. While it is important to aim high, setting unattainable goals can lead to frustration and disappointment. Assess your resources, skills, and limitations to set goals that challenge you without overwhelming you.

Lastly, it is important to review and adjust your goals regularly. Life is constantly changing, and our goals need to adapt accordingly. Regularly evaluate your progress and make necessary adjustments to stay on track.

Setting meaningful goals and ambitions is a powerful tool for personal development and growth. It provides us with a sense of purpose, fuels our motivation, and helps us become the best version of ourselves. By taking the time to reflect on our values, setting SMART goals, breaking them down into manageable steps, and regularly reviewing our progress, we can master our destiny and create a life that is truly fulfilling.

Remember, no matter who you are or what your aspirations may be, setting meaningful goals is the key to unlocking your true potential. Take charge of your destiny and start setting goals that will lead you towards a happier, more fulfilled life.

Making a Positive Impact on Others and Society

In the pursuit of personal development goals, it is crucial to recognize the profound impact we can have on others and society as a whole. Our actions and choices have the power to shape the world around us, and by consciously striving to make a positive impact, we can create a better future for everyone. Whether you are an individual seeking personal growth or a member of a team or organization, understanding the importance of this endeavor can transform your life and the lives of those around you.

One of the most effective ways to make a positive impact is by fostering empathy and compassion. By putting yourself in the shoes of others, you can gain a deeper understanding of their struggles, hopes, and dreams. This understanding enables you to offer support and encouragement, helping others navigate their own personal development journeys. By lending a helping hand, offering guidance, or simply being there to listen, you can make a significant difference in someone's life.

Another way to make a positive impact is through acts of kindness and generosity. Small gestures like volunteering your time, donating to charities, or even offering a sincere compliment can brighten someone's day and create a ripple effect of positivity. These acts not only benefit individuals but also contribute to the overall well-being of society. By fostering a culture of kindness, we can create a more compassionate and harmonious world.

Furthermore, leading by example is a powerful way to inspire others. By embodying the values and principles you believe in, you can motivate those around you to take action and make positive changes in their own lives. Whether it's practicing mindfulness, promoting sustainability, or advocating for social justice, your actions can inspire others to follow suit, creating a collective movement towards a better future.

Lastly, recognizing the interconnectedness of all beings and the environment is crucial in making a positive impact. Our choices and behaviors have consequences that extend beyond our immediate surroundings. By adopting sustainable practices, promoting equality, and being mindful of our consumption, we can contribute to a more sustainable and equitable society.

In conclusion, making a positive impact on others and society is an essential aspect of personal development goals. By fostering empathy, practicing kindness, leading by example, and recognizing our interconnectedness, we can create a better future for everyone. Whether you are an individual or part of a team, realizing the power of your actions and choices can transform not only your own life but also the lives of those around you. Together, let us strive to make a positive impact and leave a lasting legacy for generations to come.

Leaving a Lasting Legacy

In the pursuit of personal development goals, one aspect that often gets overlooked is the concept of leaving a lasting legacy. While setting and achieving personal goals is essential for individual growth, it is equally important to consider the impact we can have on others and the world around us.

Leaving a lasting legacy is not just about leaving behind material possessions or financial wealth; it is about making a positive and meaningful impact on the lives of others. It is about leaving behind a mark that will continue to inspire, motivate, and uplift generations to come.

Many individuals may question the significance of leaving a legacy, thinking that their actions may not have a lasting impact. However, it is important to remember that even small actions can create a ripple effect that could extend far beyond our lifetime. By nurturing relationships, sharing knowledge, and showing kindness, we can create a chain reaction of positivity that can shape the lives of countless individuals.

When considering how to leave a lasting legacy, it is crucial to align our actions with our values and beliefs. What is it that we truly care about? What are the causes or issues that resonate with us? By identifying these core values, we can focus our efforts on making a difference in areas that truly matter to us.

Leaving a lasting legacy also requires us to think beyond ourselves and embrace the power of collaboration. By joining forces with like-minded individuals or organizations, we can amplify our impact and create change on a larger scale. Through collective efforts, we can tackle societal challenges, address environmental issues, and promote social justice, ensuring a better future for all.

It is important to remember that leaving a lasting legacy does not happen overnight. It requires consistent effort, perseverance, and a long-term vision. By setting goals that align with our desire to leave a positive legacy, we can take meaningful steps towards creating a lasting impact.

In conclusion, leaving a lasting legacy is an integral part of personal development goals. By considering the impact we can have on others and the world around us, we can create a positive ripple effect that extends far beyond our lifetime. By aligning our actions with our values, collaborating with others, and setting long-term goals, we can leave behind a mark that inspires and uplifts generations to come. Let us strive to make a difference and leave a lasting legacy that truly matters.

Conclusion: Embracing Your Personal Development Journey

In this book, "Mastering Your Destiny: Personal Development Goals for All," we have explored the transformative power of personal development and the importance of setting goals. We have delved into various aspects of personal growth, such as self-awareness, motivation, mindset, and resilience. Now, as we reach the end of this journey, it is time to reflect on the lessons learned and embrace the path ahead.

Personal development is not a destination; it is a lifelong journey. It is a continuous process of self-improvement, self-discovery, and self-mastery. We must remember that our personal growth is unique to each one of us. No two journeys will be the same, and that is the beauty of it. Your goals and aspirations may differ from others, and that is perfectly okay.

The first step in embracing your personal development journey is self-acceptance. Understand that you are a work in progress, and it is okay to make mistakes along the way. Embrace your strengths, acknowledge your weaknesses, and be kind to yourself. Remember that personal growth is not about perfection, but about progress.

As you embark on this journey, set clear and meaningful goals. Your goals should align with your values and aspirations. Be specific, measurable, achievable, relevant, and time-bound (SMART) in setting your objectives. Break them down into smaller, manageable steps, and celebrate each milestone achieved. Remember, every small step counts towards your overall growth.

Stay motivated and maintain a positive mindset throughout your personal development journey. Surround yourself with people who uplift and inspire you. Seek out mentors, role models, and like-minded individuals who can support and guide you along the way. Cultivate a growth mindset, embrace challenges, and view setbacks as opportunities for learning and growth.

Finally, be resilient. Life is full of ups and downs, and personal development is no exception. There will be obstacles and setbacks, but it is your resilience that will determine your success. Embrace challenges as stepping stones to your personal growth and never give up on your dreams.

In conclusion, personal development is a lifelong journey that requires self-acceptance, goal setting, motivation, a positive mindset, and resilience. Embrace your uniqueness and understand that your personal growth is a continuous process. Set meaningful goals, stay motivated, seek support, and be resilient in the face of challenges. Remember, your destiny is in your hands, and by embracing your personal development journey, you can truly master your destiny.

www.ingramcontent.com/pod-product-compliance
Lightning Source LLC
LaVergne TN
LVHW051309200726
843510LV00010B/1335